I and You and
and
Don't Forget Who

What Is a Pronoun?

To my sister Maggie, who is
very much a word person.
—B.P.C.

To Wendy
—B.G.

Pronoun:
A word that
takes the place
of a noun.

NOTE: Some of the pronouns in this book are not printed in color.
As each kind of pronoun is discussed, color type highlights only the
corresponding pronouns. Can you find all of the pronouns?

I and You and and Don't Forget Who

What Is a Pronoun?

by Brian P. Cleary

illustrated by Brian Gable

CAROLRHODA BOOKS, INC. / MINNEAPOLIS

a **pronoun** steps in as
a sub for a noun,

becoming the star of the feature.

Pronouns can save us
a boatload of words
and help to avoid repetition.

They stand in for "Venice," "Marie," or "Spaghetti,"

because **that's** their specified mission.

Without **them** we'd say,
"Anne's father surprised Anne
and bought Anne
a sporty new truck.

Anne got so excited that when Anne first saw it,

Anne couldn't believe Anne's good luck."

Now, Anne is a really big
fan of her name,

but even **she'd** have to agree.

These phrases could
sure use a "her"
here and there,

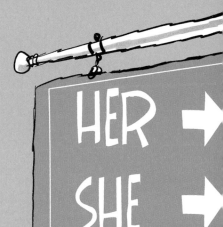

and perhaps an occasional "she."

"Personal pronouns"
stand in for a noun,

like Mrs. McKinley or Grady.

"Demonstrative pronouns"
help point something out,

as in
this, these,
and **those**
are all yours.

as in someone around
here is quite a good cook,

and something in here
smells terrific.

Nothing and all
are indefinite, too.

So are *anyone*,
no one, or any.

Everyone, none, several, somebody, some, both, neither, nobody, many.

If it helps form a question, it's called "interrogative"— a very inquisitive pronoun.

What are you looking at?
Who is your daddy?

Which road do we take
to the hoedown?

So like a pinch hitter
or a good baby-sitter,

the pronoun will say,
"You can go noun!
I've got your job covered."

So, what is a pronoun?

ABOUT THE AUTHOR & ILLUSTRATOR

BRIAN P. CLEARY is the author of the Words Are Categorical series, including A Mink, a Fink, a Skating Rink: What Is a Noun?, Hairy, Scary, Ordinary: What Is an Adjective?, and Rainbow Soup: Adventures in Poetry. He lives in Cleveland, Ohio.

BRIAN GABLE is the illustrator of Dearly, Nearly, Insincerely: What Is an Adverb? and Under, Over, By the Clover: What Is a Preposition? He lives in Toronto, Ontario, with his wife and two children.

Carolrhoda Books, Inc.,
A division of Lerner Publishing Group
241 First Avenue North
Minneapolis, MN 55401 U.S.A.

Website address: www.lernerbooks.com

Library of Congress Cataloging-in-Publication Data

Cleary, Brian P., 1959—
   I and you and don't forget who : what is a pronoun? / by Brian P. Cleary; illustrations by Brian Gable.
   p.   cm. — (Words are categorical)
   Summary: Rhyming text and illustrations of comical cats present numerous examples of pronouns and their functions, from "he" and "she" to "anyone," "neither," and "which."
   ISBN: 1-57505-808-1 (lib. bdg. : alk. paper)
   1. English language—Pronoun—Juvenile literature. [1. English language—Pronoun.] I. Gable, Brian, 1949— ill. II. Title. III. Series.
PE1261.C58 2004
   428.2—dc21   2003001712

Manufactured in the United States of America
1 2 3 4 5 6 7 — JR — 09 08 07 06 05 04